IT'S THAT TIME OF YEAR!
Raksha Bandhan
IS HERE!

BY VANESSA KAPADIA

It's That Time of Year! Raksha Bandhan is Here!

Book 2 of the It's That Time of Year Series.

Copyright © 2022 by Vanessa Kapadia

All rights reserved. No part of this book may be reproduced, distributed, or transmitted in any form or by any means, including photocopying, recording, or other electronic or mechanical methods, without prior written permission of the author, except in the case of brief quotations embodied in critical articles and reviews and certain other non-commercial uses permitted by copyright law.

ISBN

978-0-6454876-0-2 (Paperback)

978-0-6454876-1-9 (Hardcover)

978-0-6454876-2-6 (Ebook)

Dedication:

For my gorgeous niece, Dinisha, may you grow up knowing that you have the power to do and be all that you want in this life and that you are always supported and loved. Just remember to use your caring heart to guide you.

Once a year, there is a day
Where sisters visit their brothers to say -
"We will provide each other love and protection
and celebrate our special connection!"

It's That Time of Year!

Raksha Bandhan is Here!

On this day we perform a special ritual,
Which this book will teach you all.
Prepare your thali before it begins,
For that you will need a few little things.

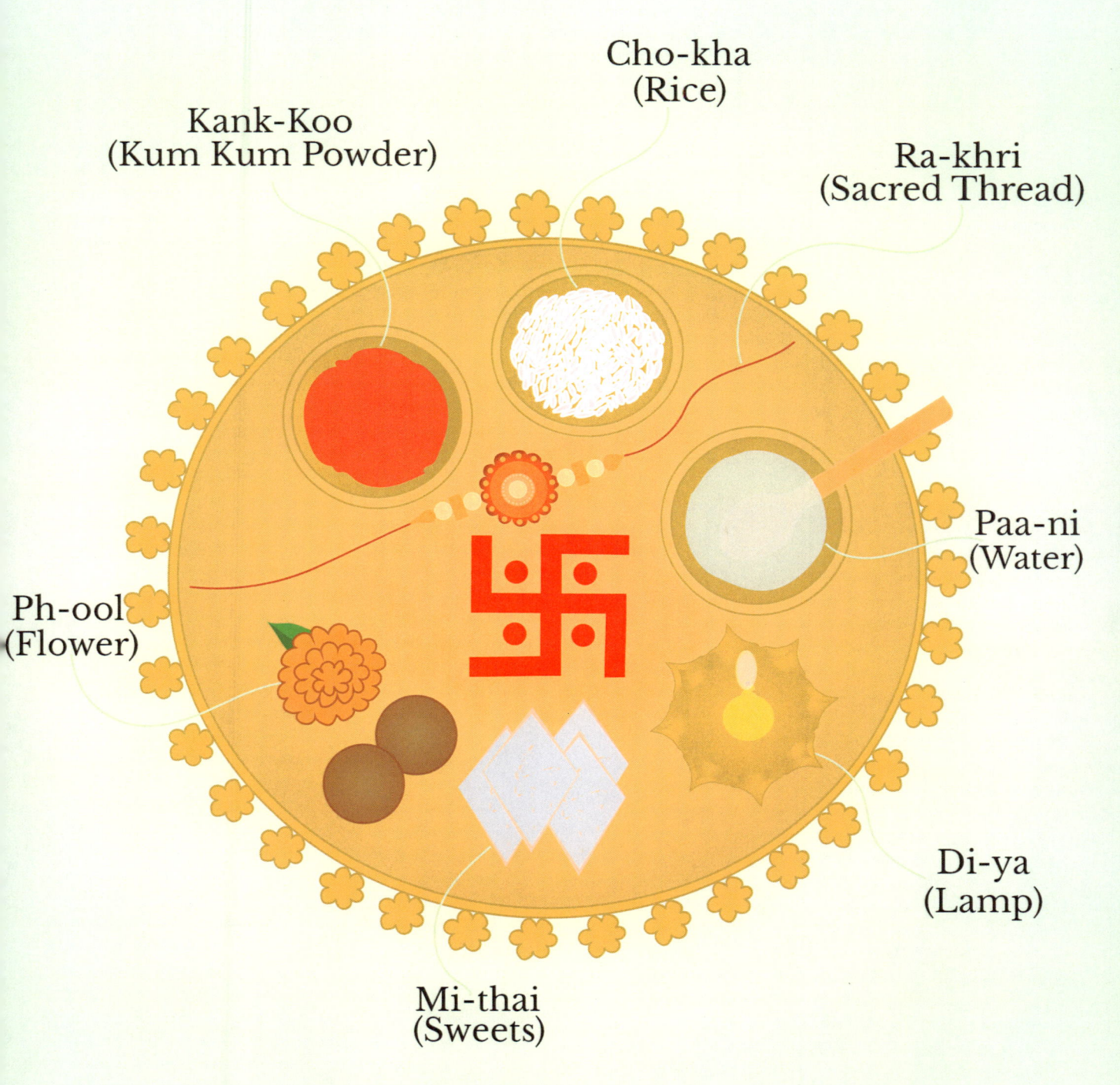

For the 1st step, the sister places a chandlo between her brother's eyebrows,

This signifies the beginning of the vows.

It connects the physical world to the spiritual.

It's a common way that we start many of our rituals.

Chandlo

How many Rakhris (Rakhis) can you see?

To make the chandlo, you'll require;
Some kum kum powder, which is red like fire.
Add a few drops of water to make a thick paste.
Then it's ready to put on his face.

Once the chandlo is in the right position,
There's one more thing to complete the tradition.
Add a few grains of rice to the chandlo and apply,
This rice will help it to purify.

The 2nd step is to perform the Arti.

The sister lights the diya on the thali.

She takes the thali clockwise three times around,

To ward off any evil that may surround.

Arti

How many Rakhris (Rakhis) can you see?

The 3rd step is for the sister to tie the Rakhri - the sacred thread.

They come in many shades but are usually red.

It's placed on the wrist that is to the right,

Looped round and round until it is tight.

As the sister gently ties it on,

She can sing this special little song.

Badhev Bandhu, Dhaan Bandhu,
Rakshey Rakshey, Maha Rakshey.
Himachal ni Putree, Parvati, Tari Raksha Karey.

She wishes good luck and success to him,

Vowing to be there through thick and thin.

Rakhri Bandhavi (Tying the Rakhri)

How many Rakhris (Rakhis) can you see?

The 4th step is oh so sweet,
When the sister feeds her brother a little treat.
It may be a delicious, special mithai,
Like Gulab Jamun, Kaju Katli or Ras Malai,
Or even a little chocolate if he prefers.
All that matters is, it's something sweet from her.

Mithai

How many Rakhris (Rakhis) can you see?

The 5th step, for tying the Rakhri on his wrist,
The brother gives his sister a special gift.
A promise of connection all year through,
It's just another way to say, "I love you."

Bheta Apavu (Gift Giving)

How many Rakhris (Rakhis) can you see?

It doesn't matter if your siblings are far away,
You can send a message, a card, or a letter their way.
Don't forget to place your Rakhri inside,
So they can wear it with pride.

If you don't have a brother or sister, please don't despair,

You can tie it on anyone as long as the feelings are there.

It could be your sister, your brother, a cousin or even a friend;

What matters most is that your love will never end.

Raksha Bandhan is such a special festival!

Stick a picture of you on Raksha Bandhan here.

What part do you love best of all?

Want to learn more about other Hindu Festivals? Then check out other titles in the series:

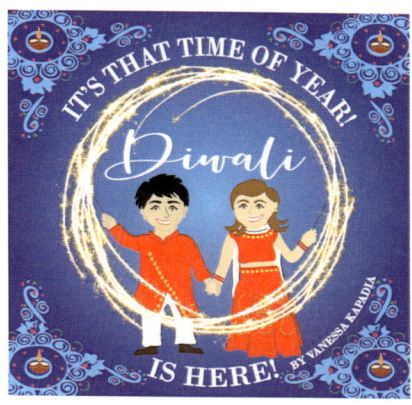

'It's That Time of Year! Diwali is Here!' (Winner of the NYC Big Book Award 2022 - Children's Religion) for a fun and simple introduction to Diwali, the 'Festival of Lights.'

Learn about the festival and the rituals of the five days of Diwali. Don't forget to find all the hidden diyas along the way.

'It's That Time of Year! Holi is Here!' for a simple explanation of the rituals performed to celebrate Holi, the 'Festival of Colours.'

Don't forget to find all the coloured objects along the way.

For more details on the book series and upcoming releases be sure to checkout the series website:

www.itsthattimeofyearseries.com

www.ingramcontent.com/pod-product-compliance
Lightning Source LLC
Chambersburg PA
CBRC090836010526
44107CB00051B/1636